The Wiersbe

BIBLE STUDY SERIES

The
Wiersbe
BIBLE STUDY SERIES

Doing

God's Will

Whatever

the Cost

David C Cook®

transforming lives together

THE WIERSBE BIBLE STUDY SERIES: RUTH AND ESTHER
Published by David C. Cook
4050 Lee Vance View
Colorado Springs, CO 80918 U.S.A.

David C. Cook Distribution Canada
55 Woodslee Avenue, Paris, Ontario, Canada N3L 3E5

David C. Cook U.K., Kingsway Communications
Eastbourne, East Sussex BN23 6NT, England

David C. Cook and the graphic circle C logo
are registered trademarks of Cook Communications Ministries.

All Scripture quotations in this study are taken from the *Holy Bible, New International Version®*. *NIV®*. Copyright © 1973, 1978, 1984 by International Bible Society. Used by permission of Zondervan. All rights reserved. Scripture quotations marked TLB are taken from *The Living Bible*, © 1971, Tyndale House Publishers, Wheaton, IL 60189. Used by permission; KJV are from the King James Version of the Bible. (Public Domain); and NKJV are taken from the New King James Version. Copyright © 1982 by Thomas Nelson, Inc. Used by permission. All rights reserved.

In the *Be Committed* excerpts, all Scripture quotations, unless otherwise noted, are taken from the *New American Standard Bible*, © Copyright 1960, 1995 by The Lockman Foundation. Used by permission. All excerpts taken from *Be Committed*, second edition, published by David C. Cook in 2008 © 1993, 2005 SP Publications, Cook Communications Ministries, ISBN 978-1-4347-6848-3

ISBN 978-0-7814-4573-3

© 2008 Warren W. Wiersbe

The Team: Steve Parolini, Gudmund Lee, Amy Kiechlin,
Jack Campbell, and Susan Vannaman
Cover Design: John Hamilton Design
Cover Photo: iStockPhoto

Printed in the United States of America
First Edition 2008

1 2 3 4 5 6 7 8 9 10

032708

Contents

Introduction to Ruth and Esther

Two Godly Women

Ruth and Esther are the only women in the Old Testament who have entire books devoted to them. The book of Ruth tells the story of a Gentile woman who married a Jew and became an ancestress of the Messiah (Matt. 1:5). The book of Esther introduces us to a Jewess who married a Gentile and was used by God to save the Jewish nation from destruction so the Messiah could be born.

The story of Ruth begins with a famine and ends with the birth of a baby, while the story of Esther begins with a feast and ends with the death of over seventy-five thousand people. God is mentioned twenty-five times in the book of Ruth, but He is not named even once in all the book of Esther! Yet in both books, the will of God is fulfilled and the providential hand of God is clearly seen.

Why do we bring these two women together in this study? Because, in spite of their differences, both Ruth and Esther were committed to do the will of God. Ruth's reply to Naomi (Ruth 1:16–17) is one of the great confessions of faith found in Scripture, and Esther's reply to Mordecai (Est. 4:16) reveals a woman willing to lay down her life to save her people. Ruth and Esther both summon Christians today to be committed to Jesus Christ and to do His will at any cost.

The Book of Ruth

The main purpose of the book of Ruth is historical. It explains the ancestry of David and builds a bridge between the time of the Judges and the period when God gave Israel a king.

This little book reveals the providence of God in the way He guided Ruth and Naomi. It encourages me to know that God still cares for us even when we're bitter toward Him, as Naomi was. God directed Ruth, a "new believer," and used her faith and obedience to transform defeat into victory. God is concerned about the details of our lives, and this fact should give us courage and joy as we seek to live each day to please Him.

The book of Ruth beautifully illustrates God's work of salvation. The story opens with Ruth as an outsider, a stranger, but it ends with Ruth as a member of the covenant community because she has married Boaz, her kinsman redeemer. He paid the price for her to be redeemed.

The book of Ruth reminds us that God is at work in our world, seeking a bride and reaping a harvest; and we must find our place in His program of winning the lost. The events in the book of Ruth occurred during the period of the Judges, a time not much different from our own day. If you focus only on the evils of our day, you'll become pessimistic and cynical; but, if you ask God what field He wants you to work in and faithfully serve Him, you'll experience His grace, love, and joy.

The Book of Esther

Ruth and Esther lived in different worlds, but the same God was present and at work in their lives, even though His name is not once mentioned in the book of Esther. "While there is no name of God, and no mention of the Hebrew religion anywhere," wrote G. Campbell Morgan, "no one reads this book without being conscious of God" (*The Living Messages of the Books of the Bible*, vol. 1, p. 269). The God of the fields in the book of Ruth is also the God of the feasts in the book of Esther. He guides the poor gleaner in the harvest and overrules the powerful king on the throne. He has His way with both of them, though He never violates their freedom.

This fact ought to encourage God's people. Whether you live on a farm, in a small town, in the suburbs, or in a metropolis, God is there and is always at work on behalf of His people. Nobody can escape the watchful eye or the faithful hand of Almighty God, for God "works all things according to the counsel of His will" (Eph. 1:11 NKJV).

One of the major themes of this book is the providence of God. Kings may issue their unalterable decrees, but God overrules and accomplishes His purposes.

But why is God not mentioned in this book? The word *king* is found over one hundred times in the book of Esther, and the name of the king nearly thirty times; but God's glorious name is not mentioned once. Is it because the Jewish nation was displeasing to God at that time and under His discipline? Perhaps.

This much is true: Though God is not named in this book, He is present and active. He was not hiding; He was only hidden. The book of Esther is one of the greatest illustrations in the Bible of Romans 8:28. God faithfully works "according to His will in the army of heaven and among the inhabitants of the earth" (Dan. 4:35 NKJV). This means that we can trust Him without fear and obey Him without hesitation, "for the kingdom is the LORD's, and He rules over the nations" (Ps. 22:28 NKJV).

God can use poor peasants and powerful queens to accomplish His divine purposes in this world. The question is not "Where do I live and work?" but "For whom do I live and work—for myself or my Lord?"

—*Warren W. Wiersbe*

How to Use This Study

This study is designed for both individual and small-group use. We've divided it into eight lessons—each references one or more chapters in Warren W. Wiersbe's commentary *Be Committed* (second edition, David C. Cook, 2008). While reading *Be Committed* is not a prerequisite for going through this study, the additional insights and background Wiersbe offers can greatly enhance your study experience.

The **Getting Started** questions at the beginning of each lesson offer you an opportunity to record your first thoughts and reactions to the study text. This is an important step in the study process as those "first impressions" often include clues about what it is your heart is longing to discover.

The bulk of the study is found in the **Going Deeper** questions. These dive into the Bible text and, along with helpful excerpts from Wiersbe's commentary, help you examine not only the original context and meaning of the verses but also modern application.

Looking Inward narrows the focus down to your personal story. These intimate questions can be a bit uncomfortable at times, but don't shy away from honesty here. This is where you are asked to stand before the mirror of God's Word and look closely at what you see. It's the place to take a good look at yourself in light of the lesson and search for ways in which you can grow in faith.

Going Forward is the place where you can commit to paper those things you want or need to do in order to better live out the discoveries you made in the Looking Inward section. Don't skip or skim through this. Take the time to really consider what practical steps you might take to move closer to Christ. Then share your thoughts with a trusted friend who can act as an encourager and accountability partner.

Finally, there is a brief **Seeking Help** section to close the lesson. This is a reminder for you to invite God into your spiritual-growth process. If you choose to write out a prayer in this section, come back to it as you work through the lesson and continue to seek the Holy Spirit's guidance as you discover God's will for your life.

Tips for Small Groups

A small group is a dynamic thing. One week it might seem like a group of close-knit friends. The next it might seem more like a group of uncomfortable strangers. A small-group leader's role is to read these subtle changes and adjust the tone of the discussion accordingly.

Small groups need to be safe places for people to talk openly. It is through shared wrestling with difficult life issues that some of the greatest personal growth is discovered. But in order for the group to feel safe, participants need to know it's okay *not* to share sometimes. Always invite honest disclosure, but never force someone to speak if he or she isn't comfortable doing so. (A savvy leader will follow up later with a group member who isn't comfortable sharing in a group setting to see if a one-on-one discussion is more appropriate.)

Have volunteers take turns reading excerpts from Scripture or from the commentary. The more each person is involved even in the mundane tasks, the more he or she will feel comfortable opening up in more meaningful ways.

Finally, soak your group meetings in prayer—before you begin, during as needed, and always at the end of your time together.

A Bad Decision
(RUTH 1)

Before you begin …
- *Pray for the Holy Spirit to reveal truth and wisdom as you go through this lesson.*
- *Read Ruth 1. This lesson references chapter 1 in* Be Committed. *It will be helpful for you to have your Bible and a copy of the commentary available as you work through this lesson.*

Getting Started

From the Commentary

"The efforts which we make to escape from our destiny only serve to lead us into it."

The American essayist Ralph Waldo Emerson wrote that in his book *The Conduct of Life*, and it's just as true today as when the book was published back in 1860. Because God gave us freedom of choice, we can ignore the will of God, argue with it, disobey it, even fight against it. But in the end, the will of God will prevail, because "He does according to His will in the army of heaven and among the inhabitants of the earth" (Dan. 4:35 NKJV).

—*Be Committed,* page 17

1. What was your immediate reaction to this first chapter of Ruth? Were Naomi's complaints justifiable?

More to Consider: You'll notice throughout this book (and the Bible in general) that names carry great significance, and that a name change is not a matter of vanity or preference, but representative of a life change. However, in this case, though Naomi wanted people to call her Mara (which means "bitter"), she is referred to consistently afterward still as Naomi. Why doesn't the writer of Ruth refer to Naomi as Mara from here forward? What does this suggest about why some name changes "stick" and others don't?

2. Choose one verse or phrase from Ruth 1 that stands out to you. This could be something you're intrigued by, something that makes you

uncomfortable, something that puzzles you, something that resonates with you, or just something you want to examine further. Write that here. What strikes you about this verse?

Going Deeper

From the Commentary

> If we obey God's will, everything in life holds together; but if we disobey, everything starts to fall apart. Nowhere in the Bible is this truth better illustrated than in the experiences of Elimelech and his wife, Naomi.
>
> —*Be Committed*, page 17

3. Circle every attempt Naomi makes to send Ruth and Orpah away to their hometowns. Why do you think Naomi is so insistent about sending them away? Do you think her determination is prompted by her grief? Why or why not? Why does she finally relent? How might God be working in her life in this exchange?

From the Commentary

> When trouble comes to our lives, we can do one of three
> things: endure it, escape it, or enlist it. If we only endure
> our trials, then trials become our master, and we have a
> tendency to become hard and bitter. If we try to escape
> our trials, then we will probably miss the purposes God
> wants to achieve in our lives. But if we learn to enlist our
> trials, they will become our servants instead of our masters
> and work for us; and God will work all things together for
> our good and His glory (Rom. 8:28).
>
> —*Be Committed*, page 19

4. Which response to trouble do you see most often in your life and the
lives of those around you? Endurance? Escape? Enlistment? Why do you
think that is? What does it look like to "enlist" trials? Can God also work
through enduring trials? Escape attempts? How?

From Today's World

The story of Naomi and Ruth is one that ultimately proves to be an example of healthy relations between in-laws. However, popular media tends to portray the relationship between adult children and their in-laws in less than flattering ways. Consider the movies or television shows you've seen that depict adult children and their mothers-in-law.

5. Why do you think people tend to expect the worst from in-law relationships? What are the greatest challenges adult children face when considering their in-laws? If Naomi's story were played out in popular media, how might Ruth's character respond differently?

From the Commentary

How do you walk by faith? By claiming the promises of God and obeying the Word of God, in spite of what you see, how you feel, or what may happen. It means committing yourself to the Lord and relying wholly on Him to meet the need. When we live by faith, it glorifies God, witnesses to a lost world, and builds Christian character into our lives. God has ordained that "the righteous will live by his faith" (Hab. 2:4; Rom. 1:17; Gal. 3:11; Heb. 10:38; 2 Cor. 5:7); and when we refuse to trust Him, we are calling God a liar and dishonoring Him.

—*Be Committed*, page 19

6. In your own words, what does it mean to "walk by faith"? When Elimelech left because of famine, do you think that was an example of walking by faith or walking by sight? In what ways does Ruth exemplify "walking by faith"? Is it possible to walk by faith when your faith hasn't even been defined? Why or why not?

More to Consider: Look up the following verses Wiersbe references: Hab. 2:4; Rom. 1:17; Gal. 3:11; Heb. 10:38; 2 Cor. 5:7. In what ways do each of these illustrate how the righteous live by faith?

From the Commentary

God visited His faithful people in Bethlehem, but not His disobedient daughter in Moab. Naomi heard the report that the famine had ended, and when she heard the good news, she decided to return home. There is always "bread enough and to spare" when you are in the Father's will (Luke 15:17 kjv). How sad it is when people only *hear* about God's blessing, but never experience it, because they are not in the place where God can bless them.…

Naomi's decision was right, but her motive was wrong. She was still interested primarily in food, not in fellowship with God. You don't hear her confessing her sins to God and asking Him to forgive her. She was returning to her land but not to her Lord.

—*Be Committed*, pages 21–22

7. What are your reactions to what Wiersbe writes in the excerpt? What sins did Naomi need to confess to God? What are some similar situations you've witnessed in your own experience about good decisions based on wrong motives? How do you think God responds to these decisions?

From the Commentary

Naomi was trying to cover up, Orpah had given up, but Ruth was prepared to stand up! She refused to listen to her mother-in-law's pleas or follow her sister-in-law's bad example. Why? *Because she had come to trust in the God of*

Israel (2:12). She had experienced trials and disappoint-ments, but instead of blaming God, she had trusted Him and was not ashamed to confess her faith. In spite of the bad example of her disobedient in-laws, Ruth had come to know the true and living God, and she wanted to be with His people and dwell in His land.

—*Be Committed*, page 24

8. Though their circumstances were very similar, Ruth and Naomi had very different responses to them. Why do you think this is true? How is this like the way Christians today respond differently to trials and disappointments? What does this say about the creative way in which God speaks to each of us through difficult times?

More to Consider: What sort of conversations do you think Naomi and Ruth had as they ventured back to Bethlehem from Moab? In what ways might Naomi's bitterness toward God have impacted their relationship?

From the Commentary

We can't control the circumstances of life, but we can control how we respond to them. That's what faith is all about, daring to believe that God is working everything for our good even when we don't feel like it or see it happening. "In everything give thanks" (1 Thess. 5:18) isn't always easy to obey, but obeying this command is the best antidote against a bitter and critical spirit. The Scottish preacher George H. Morrison said, "Nine-tenths of our unhappiness is selfishness, and is an insult cast in the face of God." Because Naomi was imprisoned by selfishness, she was bitter against God.

—*Be Committed*, page 27

9. What are some examples of being "imprisoned by selfishness" you've known or seen? How does selfishness lead to bitterness? What are the steps that a person needs to take to turn away from bitterness and instead give thanks for difficult times? What obstacles do we face when attempting to give thanks for difficult times?

From the Commentary

> Naomi thought that life had ended for her, but her trials were really a new beginning. Naomi's faith and hope were about to die, but God had other plans for her!
>
> Naomi not only had life, but she also had *opportunity*. She was surrounded by friends, all of whom wanted the very best for her. At first, her sorrow and bitterness isolated her from the community, but gradually that changed. Instead of sitting and looking gloomily at a wall, she finally decided to look out the window, and then she got up and opened the door! When the night is the darkest, if we look up, we can still see the stars.
>
> —*Be Committed*, page 28

10. Think about times when you or a friend or family member has faced trials and then discovered later that those trials were really a new beginning. How did you or the other person respond initially to the trials? What changed to help you or the other person discover the "newness"? Naomi was surrounded by friends who wanted the best for her. What does this tell us about the importance of Christian community—especially in challenging times?

Looking Inward

Take a moment to reflect on all that you've explored thus far in this study of Ruth 1. Review your notes and answers and think about how each of these things matters in your life today.

Tips for Small Groups: To get the most out of this section, form pairs or trios and have group members take turns answering these questions. Be honest and as open as you can in this discussion, but most of all, be encouraging and supportive of others. Be sensitive to those who are going through particularly difficult times and don't press for people to speak if they're uncomfortable doing so.

11. Whom do you most relate to in this chapter of Ruth: Ruth, Orpah, or Naomi? Why? What does this say about how you respond to challenging circumstances? Which person would you most *like* to relate to? What steps would you need to take to be more like her?

12. When have you felt bitter toward God? What prompted that feeling? What does it take to move from bitterness to joy?

13. As you consider the first chapter of Ruth, what thoughts do you have about your current relationship with God? If you are in a season of being distant from God, how can you move toward Him? If you are in a season of closeness, what brought you here?

Going Forward

14. Think of one or two things that you have learned that you'd like to work on in the coming week. Remember that this is all about quality, not quantity. It's better to work on one specific area of life and do it well than to work on many and do so poorly (or to be so overwhelmed that you simply don't try).

Do you need to work on overcoming bitterness? Moving close to God in difficult circumstances? What does working on this look like in practical terms? Be specific. Go back through Ruth 1 and put a star next to the phrase or verse that is most encouraging to you. Consider memorizing this verse.

Real-Life Application Ideas: Consider a bad decision you've made recently, then write down what led you to make that decision. Next, write down some thoughts about what you've learned from that decision. Has it led you closer to God? Farther from God? What are some things you think God is telling you through this circumstance? How might those lessons impact the way you deal with this bad decision (or the consequences of that decision)?

Seeking Help

15. Write a prayer below (or simply pray one in silence), inviting God to work on your mind and heart in those areas you've previously noted. Be honest about your desires and fears.

Notes for Small Groups:

- *Look for ways to put into practice the things you wrote in the "Going Forward" section. Talk with other group members about your ideas and commit to being accountable to one another.*

- *During the coming week, ask the Holy Spirit to continue to reveal truth to you from what you've read and studied.*

- *Before you start the next lesson, read Ruth 2—3. For more in-depth lesson preparation, read chapters 2 and 3, "The Greatest of These" and "The Midnight Meeting," in* Be Committed.

Love, Grace, and a New Day
(RUTH 2—3)

Before you begin ...
- *Pray for the Holy Spirit to reveal truth and wisdom as you go through this lesson.*
- *Read Ruth 2—3. This lesson references chapters 2 and 3 in* Be Committed. *It will be helpful for you to have your Bible and a copy of the commentary available as you work through this lesson.*

Getting Started

From the Commentary

Before God changes our circumstances, He wants to change our hearts. If our circumstances change for the better, but we remain the same, then we will become worse. God's purpose in providence is not to make us comfortable, but to make us conformable, "conformed to the image of His Son" (Rom. 8:29). Christlike character is the divine goal for each of His children.

—*Be Committed*, page 33

1. Respond to the *Be Committed* quote just presented. How does this speak to the content of Ruth 2—3?

More to Consider: Notice that Ruth is referred to as "Ruth the Moabitess" throughout the first few chapters of Ruth. But this changes after she marries Boaz, and she is then referred to only as Ruth. She is given a new identity that essentially redefines (if not "erases") her past. Describe how this is similar to what happens when someone becomes a believer in Christ.

2. Choose one verse or phrase from Ruth 2—3 that stands out to you. This could be something you're intrigued by, something that makes you uncomfortable, something that puzzles you, something that resonates with you, or just something you want to examine further. Write that here. What strikes you about this verse?

Going Deeper

From the Commentary

> To live by faith means to take God at His word and then act upon it, for "faith without works is dead" (James 2:20 NKJV). Since Ruth believed that God loved her and would provide for her, she set out to find a field in which she could glean. This was completely an act of faith because, being a stranger, she didn't know who owned the various parcels of ground that made up the fields. There were boundary markers for each parcel, but no fences or family name signs as seen on our farms today. Furthermore, as a woman and an outsider, she was especially vulnerable, and she had to be careful where she went.
>
> It is here that Boaz enters the story (Ruth 2:1, 3), a relative of Elimelech who was "a man of standing" (NIV) in the community.
>
> —*Be Committed*, page 34

3. Sometimes events that play out in Scripture might look at first like "coincidence" rather than providence. How is Ruth's act of faith rewarded by God? Do we always get to see the result of our faith in such a vivid way? What does this Scripture passage teach us about faith?

From the Commentary

Naomi had hope because of *who Boaz was*—a near kinsman who was wealthy and influential. As we shall see, a near kinsman could rescue relatives from poverty and give them a new beginning (Lev. 25:25–34). But she also had hope because of *what Boaz did:* He showed kindness to Ruth and took a personal interest in her situation. When Ruth shared with Naomi *what Boaz had said,* Naomi's hope grew even stronger because the words of Boaz revealed his love for Ruth and his desire to make her happy. That Boaz insisted on Ruth staying close to his servants and in his field was proof to Naomi that her husband's relative was making plans that included her and her daughter-in-law.

Should not we who believe in Jesus Christ rejoice in hope?

—*Be Committed*, page 41

4. Circle or underline all the reasons Ruth had to hope after meeting Boaz. How did God build up her hope? How is this like the way God builds hope in the lives of His followers today? What are the greatest obstacles to seeing or feeling hope?

More to Consider: Read about the evidences of God's grace in the way Boaz related to Ruth in Ruth 2:8–18. For example, Boaz took the initiative, made the first move to come to her aid, as God makes the first move toward us, too (v. 8). List all that you find.

From Today's World

There are so many different churches today that a Christian can probably find one that fits his or her greatest perceived "needs" or "wants." Skim the yellow pages or go online to find a list of churches and what they proclaim to offer Christians, and you'll find everything from a nontraditional service for seekers or those who were burned by church in the past to a traditional service complete with hymns and liturgy that hearken back to the days of Luther.

5. How does our "cafeteria-style" approach to Christianity impact the way believers go about serving Christ? How does this compare to the manner in which people like Ruth approached a life of faith in God? What are the benefits of a simpler, trusting faith (faith that focuses on worshipping God) versus a faith that seeks comfort or familiarity (faith that focuses on meeting needs)? What lessons can we learn about worship from Ruth's faith?

From the Commentary

> Ever since Boaz came into Ruth's life, Naomi has been
> a different person. Her concern is no longer for herself
> and her grief but for Ruth and her future. *It's when we
> serve others that we ourselves receive the greatest joy and
> satisfaction.* The martyred German minister Dietrich
> Bonhoeffer called Jesus Christ "the man for others," and
> the title is appropriate. "Be humble, thinking of others
> as better than yourself. Don't just think about your own
> affairs, but be interested in others, too, and in what they
> are doing" (Phil. 2:3–4 TLB).
>
> —*Be Committed*, page 47

6. Why does Boaz's relationship with Ruth impact Naomi so power-
fully? What are other ways a simple act of service can impact those who
observe that act? What does this suggest about the manner in which
Christians ought to relate to those around them at all times? How have
you been influenced or encouraged by the service of another?

More to Consider: Wiersbe writes, "Grace is love that pays the price to help the undeserving one." What is your reaction to this definition? How have you seen this enacted in the lives of those around you?

From the Commentary

> Keep in mind that the book of Ruth is much more than the record of the marriage of a rejected alien to a respected Jew. It's also the picture of Christ's relationship to those who trust Him and belong to Him. In the steps that Ruth takes, recorded in this chapter, we see the steps God's people must take if they want to enter into a deeper relationship with the Lord.
>
> —*Be Committed*, pages 47–48

7. In what specific ways does Ruth 2—3 describe the relationship between Christ and those who trust Him? List the "steps" God's people must take to enter into a deeper relationship with Him.

From the Commentary

> If we want to enter into a deeper relationship with our
> Lord, we must "cleanse ourselves from all filthiness of
> the flesh and spirit, perfecting holiness in the fear of
> God" (2 Cor. 7:1 NKJV). Whenever we sin, we must pray,
> "Wash me" (Ps. 51:2, 7), but sometimes God says to us,
> "Wash yourselves, make yourselves clean" (Isa. 1:16
> NKJV). When we seek forgiveness, God washes the record
> clean (1 John 1:9), but God will not do for us what we
> must do for ourselves. Only we can put out of our lives
> those things that defile us, *and we know what they are.*
>
> —*Be Committed*, page 48

8. Ruth's preparation to meet Boaz was a fivefold process that included
something we take for granted: bathing. What is the significance of this
act that often precedes special events? In what ways do we need to also
cleanse ourselves, as Ruth did? What are we preparing for when we make
ourselves clean?

From the Commentary

> In the responses of Boaz to Ruth, we see how the Lord responds to us when we seek to have a deeper fellowship with Him. Just as Boaz spoke to Ruth, so God speaks to us from His Word.
>
> He accepts us [(Ruth 3:8–10)]….
>
> He assures us [(Ruth 3:11–13)].
>
> —*Be Committed,* pages 53–54

9. How do we go about "listening" to God? What are the practical steps we must take to be open to hearing His Word? How are the words that Boaz spoke to Ruth like those God speaks to us? What form do those words take? What does His acceptance look like? His assurance?

From the Commentary

> I confess that *waiting* is one of the most difficult things for me to do, whether it's waiting for a table at a restaurant or waiting for a delayed flight to take off. I'm an activist by nature, and I like to see things happen on time. Perhaps

that's why the Lord has often arranged for me to wait. During those times, three phrases from Scripture have encouraged me: "Sit still" (Ruth 3:18 NKJV), "Stand still" (Ex. 14:13 NKJV), and "Be still" (Ps. 46:10 NKJV).

—*Be Committed*, pages 56–57

10. Naomi was the person who counseled Ruth to "sit still" and wait. Why do you think Naomi chose this bit of advice for Ruth? In what ways was Ruth living out her story "in faith and patience"? Why is patience so difficult for us? How is strength found in patience?

Looking Inward

Take a moment to reflect on all that you've explored thus far in this study of Ruth 2—3. Review your notes and answers and think about how each of these things matters in your life today.

Tips for Small Groups: To get the most out of this section, form pairs or trios and have group members take turns answering these questions. Be honest and as open as you can in this discussion, but most of all, be encouraging and supportive of others. Be sensitive to those who are going through particularly difficult times and don't press for people to speak if they're uncomfortable doing so.

11. How would you describe your level of faith today? What are some ways your faith is like Ruth's? What arc some things you could learn from Ruth's faith?

12. Ruth had many reasons to hope. What are the signs in your life that give you reason to hope? What are the things you are hoping for?

13. Remember Ruth's preparation to meet Boaz? What things do you need to do to prepare your heart before Christ? Are these easy to do? Why or why not?

Going Forward

14. Think of one or two things that you have learned that you'd like to work on in the coming week. Remember that this is all about quality, not quantity. It's better to work on one specific area of life and do it well than to work on many and do so poorly (or to be so overwhelmed that you simply don't try).

Do you need to learn to trust God more? Do you need to find the places where God is sending you a message of hope? How do you go about building the patience necessary to let God work through your circumstances? Go back through Ruth 2—3 and put a star next to the phrase or verse that speaks to your greatest areas of need when it comes to building a greater faith. Consider memorizing this verse.

Real-Life Application Ideas: Patience is a difficult thing especially when we're in the midst of trying times. Think of something you're trusting God for and write it here. Then list ways you can prepare your heart for God's answer as well as practical things you can do as you await His response to your circumstance.

Seeking Help

15. Write a prayer below (or simply pray one in silence), inviting God to work on your mind and heart in those areas you've previously noted. Be honest about your desires and fears.

Notes for Small Groups:

- *Look for ways to put into practice the things you wrote in the "Going Forward" section. Talk with other group members about your ideas and commit to being accountable to one another.*

- *During the coming week, ask the Holy Spirit to continue to reveal truth to you from what you've read and studied.*

- *Before you start the next lesson, read Ruth 4. For more in-depth lesson preparation, read chapter 4, "Love Finds a Way," in* Be Committed.

A Full Heart
(RUTH 4)

Before you begin ...
- *Pray for the Holy Spirit to reveal truth and wisdom as you go through this lesson.*
- *Read Ruth 4. This lesson references chapter 4 in* Be Committed. *It will be helpful for you to have your Bible and a copy of the commentary available as you work through this lesson.*

Getting Started

From the Commentary

The book of Ruth opens with three funerals but closes with a wedding. There is a good deal of weeping recorded in the first chapter, but the last chapter records an overflowing of joy in the little town of Bethlehem. "Weeping may endure for a night, but joy cometh in the morning" (Ps. 30:5 KJV). Not all of life's stories have this kind of happy ending, but this little book reminds us that, for the

Christian, *God still writes the last chapter.* We don't have to be afraid of the future.

—*Be Committed,* page 61

1. What is your first response to the resolution of Ruth's story? In what ways are you inspired by the happy ending?

More to Consider: Read Leviticus 25:25–34 to learn more about the law of the kinsman redeemer and Deuteronomy 25:5–10 to learn more about the law governing levirate marriage. What was the purpose of these laws? How do they impact Ruth's story?

2. Choose one verse or phrase from Ruth 4 that stands out to you. This could be something you're intrigued by, something that makes you uncomfortable, something that puzzles you, something that resonates with you, or just something you want to examine further. Write that here. What strikes you about this verse?

Going Deeper

3. Underline all the times the word *redeem* or *redeemer* are listed in Ruth 4. Describe their use. What does this tell you about the importance of redemption?

From the Commentary

> The word *redeem* means "to set free by paying a price." In the case of Ruth and Naomi, Elimelech's property had either been sold or was under some kind of mortgage, and the rights to the land had passed to Ruth's husband, Mahlon, when Elimelech died. This explains why Ruth was also involved in the transaction. She was too poor, however, to redeem the land.
>
> —*Be Committed*, page 62

4. What is your reaction to the definition of *redeem* Wiersbe gives in the excerpt? What examples of redemption are found in everyday life? Has the power of redemption gained or lost meaning since the time of Ruth? Explain.

More to Consider: Read about the redemption we have because of the blood of Christ (see 1 Peter 1:18–19; Ps. 49:5–9). How is Ruth's redemption a foreshadowing of our redemption in Christ?

From the Commentary

> In order to qualify, the kinsman-redeemer also *had to be able to pay the redemption price.* Ruth and Naomi were too poor to redeem themselves, but Boaz had all the resources necessary to set them free. When it comes to the redemption of sinners, nobody but Jesus Christ is rich enough to pay the price.
>
> —*Be Committed,* page 63

5. Why is only Jesus "rich enough" to pay the price for the redemption of sinners? What did we gain from Jesus' redemption?

From Today's World

Though the concept of "redemption" is generally missing from popular culture, people in the limelight are constantly trying to "redeem themselves" from acts that have put them in a less-than-positive light. A quick scan of the entertainment pages (or even a few minutes spent watching the nightly news) usually unearths at least one example of a celebrity who is heading to rehab (or simply trying to spin his or her actions in such a way as to right or explain away a wrong action or poor choice).

6. What does our society teach implicitly about the process of "redemption" through these celebrity stories? Can we redeem ourselves of bad choices? Is such a redemption sufficient? How is this different from being redeemed of sinful actions?

From the Commentary

> *There can be no redemption without the paying of a price.* From our point of view, salvation is free to "whosoever shall call on the name of the Lord" (Acts 2:21 KJV), but from God's point of view, redemption is a very costly thing.
>
> —*Be Committed*, page 63

7. Why is it important to our story that salvation is a free gift? What is the ultimate cost of redemption to God?

From the Commentary

> One of the many images of the church in the Bible is "the bride of Christ." In Ephesians 5:22–33, the emphasis is on Christ's love for the church as seen in His ministries: He died for the church (past), He cleanses and nourishes the church through the Word (present), and He will one day present the church in glory (future). Christ is preparing a beautiful home for His bride and one day will celebrate His wedding (Rev. 19:1–10; 21—22).
>
> —*Be Committed*, page 66

8. What does the story of Ruth teach us about the "bride of Christ"? How does her "new beginning" mirror that which we gain as Christ-followers?

From the Commentary

God would use this baby to be a source of blessing to many....

Obed was a blessing to Boaz and Ruth....

Obed was also a blessing to Naomi....

Obed would bring blessing to Bethlehem ...

Obed would bring blessing to the whole world.

—*Be Committed*, pages 67–68

9. In what ways was Ruth's son Obed a blessing to them? To Naomi? To Bethlehem? To the entire world? Why is this important to us today?

More to Consider: Wiersbe writes, "The greatest thing God did for David was not to give him victory over his enemies or wealth for the building of the temple. The greatest privilege God gave him was that of being the ancestor of the Messiah." What are your reactions to this statement? How does this also elevate Ruth's role in history (since one of her grandson's children would become David the king)?

10. Reread Ruth 4:13–22. What is the significance of the statement that "the Lord enabled her to conceive"? Why did the women say to Naomi "your daughter-in-law … is better to you than seven sons"? How does your understanding of this statement change in light of the ancient cultural importance of having sons rather than daughters? Why is the genealogy of David so important in Scripture?

Looking Inward

Take a moment to reflect on all that you've explored thus far in this study of Ruth 4. Review your notes and answers and think about how each of these things matters in your life today.

Tips for Small Groups: To get the most out of this section, form pairs or trios and have group members take turns answering these questions. Be honest and as open as you can in this discussion, but most of all, be encouraging and supportive of others. Be sensitive to those who are going through particularly difficult times and don't press for people to speak if they're uncomfortable doing so.

11. What does it mean to you that God has redeemed you? How does the story of Ruth help you understand this redemption?

12. In what ways have you tried to "redeem yourself" in life? What are the results of those attempts? Why is Jesus' sacrifice necessary for your redemption?

13. What does it look like for you to be the "bride of Christ?" What steps do you take in life to prepare for the wedding?

Going Forward

14. Think of one or two things that you have learned that you'd like to work on in the coming week. Remember that this is all about quality, not quantity. It's better to work on one specific area of life and do it well than to work on many and do so poorly (or to be so overwhelmed that you simply don't try).

Do you need to stop trying to redeem yourself? Do you need to learn what it means to be the bride of Christ? Perhaps you are feeling a specific prompting to live out some truth you've discovered in the Bible. Write these thoughts below. Be specific. Go back through Ruth 4 and put a star next to the verse that is most convicting to you. Consider memorizing this verse.

Real-Life Application Ideas: Spend time in the Bible this week learning what it means to be redeemed by Christ. Use a concordance to look up the words redeem *and* redemption *and then consider how your redemption should impact your daily living. What does it mean to live a redeemed life?*

Seeking Help

15. Write a prayer below (or simply pray one in silence), inviting God to work on your mind and heart in those areas you've previously noted. Be honest about your desires and fears.

Notes for Small Groups:

- *Look for ways to put into practice the things you wrote in the "Going Forward" section. Talk with other group members about your ideas and commit to being accountable to one another.*

- *During the coming week, ask the Holy Spirit to continue to reveal truth to you from what you've read and studied.*

- *Before you start the next lesson, read Esther 1. For more in-depth lesson preparation, read chapter 5, "The Queen Says 'No!'" in* Be Committed.

The

Disagreement
(ESTHER 1)

Before you begin ...
- *Pray for the Holy Spirit to reveal truth and wisdom as you go through this lesson.*
- *Read Esther 1. This lesson references chapter 5 in* Be Committed. *It will be helpful for you to have your Bible and a copy of the commentary available as you work through this lesson.*

Getting Started

From the Commentary

> Like most monarchs of that day, Ahasuerus was a proud man, and in this chapter, we see three evidences of his pride.
>
> —*Be Committed*, page 83

1. What was your initial reaction to King Ahasuerus's decisions? What evidences of pride did you see in Esther 1?

More to Consider: Review the display of power and wealth described in Esther 1:4–8. Why do you think this is included in Esther? How does this set the stage for the story that follows?

2. Choose one verse or phrase from Esther 1 that stands out to you. This could be something you're intrigued by, something that makes you uncomfortable, something that puzzles you, something that resonates with you, or just something you want to examine further. Write that here. What strikes you about this verse?

Going Deeper

From the Commentary

If ever a man should have learned the truth of Proverbs 16:18, it was Ahasuerus: "Pride goes before destruction, and a haughty spirit before a fall" (NKJV).

People in authority need to remember that all authority comes from God (Rom. 13:1) and that He alone is in complete control. Pharaoh had to learn that lesson in Egypt (Ex. 7:3–5); Nebuchadnezzar had to learn it in Babylon (Dan. 3—4); Belshazzar learned it at his blasphemous banquet

(Dan. 5); Sennacherib learned it at the gates of Jerusalem (Isa. 36—37); and Herod Agrippa I learned it as he died, being eaten by worms (Acts 12:20–23). Every man or woman in a place of authority is second in command, for Jesus Christ is Lord of all.

—*Be Committed,* page 85

3. Briefly review the stories Wiersbe references in the excerpt. How are these examples similar to King Ahasuerus's situation? Though there is no evidence of "destruction" in this chapter, the implications are clear that he's heading for some kind of fall. Why do people with great power seem blind to these inevitable truths?

From the Commentary

As you study the book of Esther, you will discover that this mighty monarch could control everything but himself. His advisers easily influenced him; he made impetuous decisions that he later regretted; and when he didn't get his own way, he became angry. Susceptible to flattery, he was master of a mighty empire but not master of himself. "He who is slow to anger is better than the mighty, and he who rules his spirit, than he who captures a city" (Prov. 16:32). Ahasuerus built a great citadel at Shushan, but he couldn't build his own character.

—*Be Committed*, page 86

4. What might the king's empire have looked like had he built his character instead of a great city? Why is it harder to build character than wealth? What are examples of this lifestyle you've seen in today's society? What is our role as Christians when we face an "empire" like one of these?

More to Consider: Wiersbe writes, "While we appreciate the king's wisdom in not forcing his guests to drink (Est. 1:8), we can hardly compliment him on the bad example he set by his own drinking habits." Apart from a discussion about the biblical perspective on drinking, what does this tell us about the importance of setting a good example? About the influence a leader has over his people? What are some examples in today's society that underline these truths?

From the Commentary

> Vashti was right, and Ahasuerus was wrong, and his anger
> was only further proof that he was wrong. Anger has a way
> of blinding our eyes and deadening our hearts to that
> which is good and noble. The Italian poet Pietro Aletino
> (1492–1557) wrote to a friend, "Angry men are blind and
> foolish, for reason at such a time takes flight and, in her
> absence, wrath plunders all the riches of the intellect, while
> the judgment remains the prisoner of its own pride." If
> anybody was a prisoner of pride, it was the exalted king of
> the Persian Empire!
>
> —*Be Committed,* pages 87–88

5. In what ways did the king express his anger? What caused his anger?
Describe situations where you've seen a similar expression of anger. Why
are angry people "blind and foolish"? Does all anger lead to foolishness?
What is the difference between righteous anger and nonrighteous anger?

From Today's World

Excessive living is the focal point of more than a few television shows. You
can find programs showcasing everything from the homes and lifestyles of

the famous to the kinds of "toys" rich people buy. Also, nearly every celebrity exposé highlights examples of excess lived out by the star. While some celebrities like to deflect attention and focus on worthy causes, most seem to embrace the lavish, bigger-than-life lifestyle coveted by their fans.

6. What is your immediate emotional reaction to examples of excessive living in today's society? Are you compelled to see how the wealthy live? Why or why not? What are the greatest downfalls of wealth and power? Describe some examples of this. What role does pride play in these people's lives? Can someone be wealthy and not suffer from issues of pride? Explain.

From the Commentary

> Pride feeds anger, and as it grows, anger reinforces pride.
> "A quick-tempered man acts foolishly," warned the writer
> of Proverbs 14:17, a text perfectly illustrated by King Aha-
> suerus. Instead of being angry at Vashti, the king should
> have been angry at himself for acting so foolishly.
> —*Be Committed,* page 88

7. Why do people turn their anger toward others instead of themselves? What might have been different in this story had the king recognized his

own foolishness? Describe some examples in your life or the lives of those around you that illustrate the results of misdirected anger.

From the Commentary

> When the ego is pricked, it releases a powerful poison that makes people do all sorts of things they'd never do if they were humble and submitted to the Lord. Francis Bacon wrote in his *Essays,* "A man that studies revenge keeps his own wounds green, which otherwise would heal and do well." Had Ahasuerus sobered up and thought the matter through, he would never have deposed his wife. After all, she showed more character than he did.
>
> —*Be Committed,* pages 88–89

8. What is your reaction to the quote from Francis Bacon? Why is revenge such a powerful attraction for people who believe they've been wronged? How might the story have played out had the king not responded with revenge but with a desire in understanding the queen's decision? How should he have confronted her about his disappointment? What does this teach us about our own approach to those circumstances when we feel we've been wronged?

From the Commentary

> The seven wise men advised the king to depose Vashti and
> replace her with another queen. They promised that such
> an act would put fear into the hearts of all the women in
> the empire and generate more respect for their husbands.
> But would it? Are hearts changed because kings issue
> decrees or congresses and parliaments pass laws? How
> would the punishment of Vashti make the Persian women
> love their husbands more? Are love and respect qualities
> that can be generated in hearts by human fiat?
>
> —*Be Committed,* page 90

9. The solution offered by the advisers was meant to give a "message" to
the women in the empire. Instead, it ultimately leads to a very different
sort of message—one that highlighted the value and importance of
women (through Esther's story). How does the advisers' attempt to legislate love and respect play into the ultimate result? What are other
examples of attempts to change the hearts of men and women through
external measures?

From the Commentary

> Still motivated by anger and revenge, and seeking to heal
> his wounded pride, the king agreed to their advice and
> had Vashti deposed (Est. 1:19–21). He sent his couriers
> throughout the empire to declare the royal edict—an edict
> that was unnecessary, unenforceable, and unchangeable.
> King Ahasuerus was given to issuing edicts, and he didn't
> always stop to think about what he was doing (3:9–12). It
> was another evidence of his pride.
>
> —*Be Committed*, page 90

10. Why did the king issue edicts that were unenforceable? Have you seen
similar expressions of pride or power in your own life? At work? Among
friends? At school? How are Christians supposed to respond to authorities
who issue "edicts" that have potentially negative consequences?

Looking Inward

Take a moment to reflect on all that you've explored thus far in this study
of Esther 1. Review your notes and answers and think about how each of
these things matters in your life today.

Tips for Small Groups: To get the most out of this section, form pairs or trios and have group members take turns answering the following questions. Be honest and as open as you can in this discussion, but most of all, be encouraging and supportive of others. Be sensitive to those who are going through particularly difficult times and don't press for people to speak if they're uncomfortable doing so.

11. Consider your own circumstances and influence. Do you ever act out of pride or vengeance? What prompts that response? Does power or wealth play into your pride? In what ways?

12. How do you deal with anger? Think of a time when you reacted out of anger inappropriately, perhaps harming another in the process. What led to that reaction? What would have been a better response? Now think of a time when you were angry but didn't act wrongly in that anger. What's the difference between these two situations? How does your relationship with Christ impact the way you respond when something makes you angry?

13. Have you ever felt as if someone was attempting to "legislate" your feelings or character? How did you deal with that? What is a Christlike response when someone in authority is attempting to direct your heart?

Going Forward

14. Think of one or two things you have learned that you'd like to work on in the coming week. Remember that this is all about quality, not quantity. It's better to work on one specific area of life and do it well than to work on many and do so poorly (or to be so overwhelmed that you simply don't try).

Do you need to work on your pride? Your anger? A vengeful spirit? Perhaps you are feeling a specific prompting to take action on some truth you've discovered while doing this lesson. Write these thoughts below. Be specific. Go back through Esther 1 and put a star next to the verse that speaks to the area you most need to work on. Consider memorizing this verse.

Real-Life Application Ideas: Note all the areas in your life where you have power or influence over others. Then do a self-evaluation to see if you are acting out of pride or anger in any of those areas. If so, consider if you need to apologize to anyone (do so) and if you need to change your approach to leadership so you are not acting pridefully.

Seeking Help

15. Write a prayer below (or simply pray one in silence), inviting God to work on your mind and heart in those areas you've previously noted. Be honest about your desires and fears.

Notes for Small Groups:
- *Look for ways to put into practice the things you wrote in the "Going Forward" section. Talk with other group members about your ideas and commit to being accountable to one another.*
- *During the coming week, ask the Holy Spirit to continue to reveal truth to you from what you've read and studied.*
- *Before you start the next lesson, read Esther 2—3. For more in-depth lesson preparation, read chapters 6 and 7, "The New Queen" and "An Old Enemy with a New Name," in* Be Committed.

The New Queen
(ESTHER 2—3)

Before you begin ...
- *Pray for the Holy Spirit to reveal truth and wisdom as you go through this lesson.*
- *Read Esther 2—3. This lesson references chapters 6 and 7 in* Be Committed. *It will be helpful for you to have your Bible and a copy of the commentary available as you work through this lesson.*

Getting Started

From the Commentary

"God is preparing His heroes," said A. B. Simpson, founder of the Christian and Missionary Alliance, "and when the opportunity comes, He can fit them into their places in a moment, and the world will wonder where they came from."

Dr. Simpson might have added that God also prepares His *heroines,* for certainly Esther was divinely prepared for her role as the new queen. *God is never surprised by circum-stances or at a loss for prepared servants.* He had Joseph ready in Egypt (Ps. 105:17), Ezekiel and Daniel in Babylon, and Nehemiah in Susa; and He had Esther ready for her ministry to the Jews in the Persian Empire.

—*Be Committed*, page 95

1. How do you feel when you read that "God is preparing His heroes (and heroines)"? Does this inspire you? Humble you? What if you're one of the heroes or heroines God is preparing?

More to Consider: Consider the heroes and heroines in your own life. Perhaps these are family members or friends or coworkers. In what ways did God prepare them to have an impact in your life?

2. Choose one verse or phrase from Esther 2—3 that stands out to you. This could be something you're intrigued by, something that makes you uncomfortable, something that puzzles you, something that resonates with

you, or just something you want to examine further. Write that here. What strikes you about this verse?

Going Deeper

From the Commentary

"The king's heart is in the hand of the LORD, like the rivers of water; He turns it wherever He wishes" (Prov. 21:1 NKJV). This doesn't mean that God forced Ahasuerus to accept the plan or that God approved of the king's harems or of his sensual abuse of women. It simply means that, without being the author of their sin, God so directed the people in this situation that decisions were made that accomplished His purposes.

—*Be Committed,* pages 96–97

3. What are your reactions to Wiersbe's thoughts? What are some other examples of God directing the people's actions in order to accomplish His purposes? How do you balance this sovereignty of God with the free will He grants all people?

From the Commentary

> When you consider the backslid state of the Jewish nation
> at that time, the disobedience of the Jewish remnant in the
> Persian Empire, and the unspiritual lifestyle of Mordecai
> and Esther, is it any wonder that the name of God is absent
> from this book? Would you want to identify your holy
> name with such an unholy people?
>
> —*Be Committed,* page 100

4. Even though God is not mentioned in Esther, His presence is certainly
evident. Are there any evidences of God in chapters 2 and 3? Circle any
you find. If not, what do you think is the purpose of these two chapters in
the larger story?

From the Commentary

> Had Esther not been born into the Jewish race, she could
> never have saved the nation from slaughter. It would appear
> that the two cousins' silence about their nationality was

directed by God because He had a special work for them
to accomplish.

—*Be Committed,* page 100

5. What do you think about God's direction of Esther's and Mordecai's "silence"? What are some other examples of God working in "mysterious ways" to accomplish His goals?

More to Consider: Read Esther 2:12, 16; and 3:7. If at any time during these events Esther had practiced her Jewish faith, she would have been "found out." Wiersbe notes this and quotes Matthew Henry who says, "All truths are not to be spoken at all times." What is your reaction to this? How do you know when it's best not to speak the truth at a given time? How is this different from lying?

From Today's World

Pick up the paper or look through the history books and you'll find plenty of examples where public officials chose not to tell the truth about a given situation. Yet the secrets that are revealed during election years can have a damaging effect on the candidates' campaigns. Some try to deny allegations, some simply accept the truth, and others attempt to confuse the circumstances with creative spin. Some of the revealed secrets are old news and have little relevance to the person's current bid for office, while others clearly have significance.

6. How are these revealed secrets like or unlike the secrets that Mordecai and Esther held while in the royal courts? Should some secrets simply be left as secrets? How do you determine which ones are okay to remain concealed? What, if any, sorts of "subterfuge" are acceptable for Christians? How can God use such things even in today's society to further His kingdom?

From the Commentary

> Mordecai received neither recognition nor reward for saving the king's life. No matter; God saw to it that the facts were permanently recorded, and He would make good use of them at the right time. Our good works are like seeds that are planted by faith, and their fruits don't always appear immediately.
>
> —*Be Committed,* pages 103–4

7. What are some other examples of people who have done great things for the faith and have seemingly gone unrewarded for their work? What are some of the seeds that have been planted by faith in your life or the lives of those around you? What are some of the seeds you've planted? How does it feel to know that you may not reap any benefits of the seed planting until after death?

From the Commentary

Everything about Haman is hateful; you can't find one thing about this man worth praising. In fact, everything about Haman *God hated!* "These six things the LORD hates, yes, seven are an abomination to Him: A proud look, a lying tongue, hands that shed innocent blood, a heart that devises wicked plans, feet that are swift in running to evil, a false witness who speaks lies, and one who sows discord among brethren" (Prov. 6:16–19 NKJV). Keep these seven evil characteristics in mind as you read the book of Esther, for you will see them depicted in this depraved man.

—*Be Committed,* pages 108–9

8. What characters in history can you think of who remind you of Haman? What are their similar motivations? What does this tell you about the nature of evil? What should a Christian's response be to such an evil person?

From the Commentary

> At some time between the seventh and twelfth years of the reign of Ahasuerus (v. 7; 2:16), the king decided to make Haman chief officer in the empire. Think of it: Mordecai had saved the king's life and didn't receive a word of thanks, let alone a reward, but wicked Haman did nothing and was promoted! There are many seeming injustices in this life, yet God knows what He's doing and will never forsake the righteous or leave their deeds unrewarded. (See Ps. 37.)
>
> —*Be Committed,* page 109

9. You probably have seen examples of injustices like the one against Mordecai. Describe one of these. Why do undeserving people often seem to get rewarded while good people are overlooked? At the end of Esther, we learn that Haman gets his "just desserts" for his evil intent. But this isn't always the case in real life. What should our response be when injustice wins out?

More to Consider: Read about the Hebrew midwives in Exodus 1:15–22; Daniel and his three friends in Daniel 1; and the apostles in Acts 5:29. How are these stories similar to Mordecai's "civil disobedience" against Haman?

From the Commentary

> Haman could send out the death warrants for thousands of innocent people and then sit down to a banquet with the king! What a calloused heart he had! He was like the people the prophet Amos described: "that drink wine in bowls, and anoint themselves with the chief ointments: but they are not grieved for the affliction of Joseph" (Amos 6:6 KJV). However, in the end, it was his own death warrant that Haman had sealed, for within less than three months, Haman would be a dead man (Est. 7:9–10; 8:9–11).
>
> Helen Keller said, "Science may have found a cure for most evils, but it has found no remedy for the worst of them all—the apathy of human beings" (*My Religion,* 162).
>
> —*Be Committed,* page 117

10. Now that you've spent some time with Haman, what is your opinion of him? If Haman (or someone like him) were suddenly hired as your boss, how would you feel? What would you do? What are some examples from your own life experiences that support what Helen Keller says about apathy? What is the cure for apathy?

Looking Inward

Take a moment to reflect on all that you've explored thus far in this study of Esther 2—3. Review your notes and answers and think about how each of these things matters in your life today.

Tips for Small Groups: To get the most out of this section, form pairs or trios and have group members take turns answering these questions. Be honest and as open as you can in this discussion, but most of all, be encouraging and supportive of others. Be sensitive to those who are going through particularly difficult times and don't press for people to speak if they're uncomfortable doing so.

11. Though God is not mentioned in Esther, His presence is clearly evident. What does this tell you about God's role in your daily life? Describe times when you don't see or hear God but know He's actively involved in your circumstances.

12. In Esther's story, God seemed to direct her to remain silent on issues that could have otherwise led to the potential destruction of the Jewish nation. Obviously, God had great plans that required the continued existence of the Jews. Think about your own life and relationships. Are there

situations where your silence about your faith could actually lead to a positive outcome—one that ultimately glorifies God? How might God use those moments?

13. Think about the circumstances in your life where you're in a position of leadership. Now consider the "seven things" that are an abomination to God (see p. 75). Are you guilty of any of these? If so, what actions do you need to take to change those things about yourself?

Going Forward

14. Think of one or two things that you have learned that you'd like to work on in the coming week. Remember that this is all about quality, not quantity. It's better to work on one specific area of life and do it well than to work on many and do so poorly (or to be so overwhelmed that you simply don't try).

Do you need to work on trusting God's creative use of your circumstances? Do you need to learn patience about seeds you've planted? Perhaps you are feeling a specific prompting to live out some truth you've discovered in the Bible. Write these thoughts below. Be specific. Go back through Esther 2—3 and put a star next to the verse that means the most to you. Consider memorizing this verse.

> *Real-Life Application Ideas: Take inventory of the difficult circumstances you're facing today because of the leadership or influence of someone in authority. How are you currently dealing with those circumstances? Spend time in prayer about them, asking God for wisdom in knowing when to speak and when to stay silent.*

Seeking Help

15. Write a prayer below (or simply pray one in silence), inviting God to work on your mind and heart in those areas you've previously noted. Be honest about your desires and fears.

Notes for Small Groups:

- *Look for ways to put into practice the things you wrote in the "Going Forward" section. Talk with other group members about your ideas and commit to being accountable to one another.*

- *During the coming week, ask the Holy Spirit to continue to reveal truth to you from what you've read and studied.*

- *Before you start the next lesson, read Esther 4—5. For more in-depth lesson preparation, read chapters 8 and 9, "A Day of Decision" and "A Day in the Life of the Prime Minister," in* Be Committed.

Decisions
(ESTHER 4—5)

Before you begin …
- *Pray for the Holy Spirit to reveal truth and wisdom as you go through this lesson.*
- *Read Esther 4—5. This lesson references chapters 8 and 9 in* Be Committed. *It will be helpful for you to have your Bible and a copy of the commentary available as you work through this lesson.*

Getting Started

From the Commentary

Mordecai's appearance and actions (v. 1) were those of a person showing great grief (2 Sam. 1:11–12; 13:19) or deep repentance (Jonah 3; Neh. 9:1–2). Mordecai was neither afraid nor ashamed to let people know where he stood. He had already told the officers at the gate that he was a Jew; now he was telling the whole city that he was not only a Jew but also that he opposed the murderous edict. Although it can't be documented from his writings, a statement usually attributed to the British politician Edmund Burke certainly applies here: "All that is required for evil to triumph is for good men to do nothing."

—*Be Committed,* pages 121–22

1. What do you think of Mordecai's decisions and actions in this chapter? In what ways was his ability to speak confidently and unashamedly the result of God's timing or providence?

More to Consider: What do you think of Esther's initial response to Mordecai's actions at the gate? She didn't immediately ask Mordecai what the problem was but instead tried to solve it by sending him fine clothes so he wouldn't "stand out" and become the object of concern. How is this like the way we often try to hide things rather than deal with them directly?

2. Choose one verse or phrase from Esther 4—5 that stands out to you. This could be something you're intrigued by, something that makes you uncomfortable, something that puzzles you, something that resonates with

you, or just something you want to examine further. Write that here. What strikes you about this verse?

Going Deeper

From the Commentary

> As you ponder Mordecai's words, you will learn some basic truths about the providence of God that are important for Christians today. The first is that *God has divine purposes to accomplish in this world.* God's purposes involve the Jewish nation as well as the Gentile nations of the world. They also involve the church. God deals with individuals as well as with nations. His purposes touch the lives of kings and queens and common people, godly people and wicked people. There is nothing in this world that is outside the influence of the purposes of God.
>
> —*Be Committed,* page 126

3. Underline things in chapters 4—5 that suggest God's providence is at work. What are some examples of God using the lives of both godly and

ungodly people to accomplish His purposes? Where do you see this happening today?

From the Commentary

> God is never in a hurry. He knows the end from the beginning, and His decrees are always right and always on time. Dr. A. W. Tozer compared God's sovereign purposes to an ocean liner leaving New York City, bound for Liverpool, England. The people on board the ship are free to do as they please, but they aren't free to change the course of the ship.
>
> —*Be Committed,* page 127

4. What is your response to Tozer's comment about God's sovereign purposes? In what ways do you see this truth in the church today? How can this reframe difficult or confusing life experiences people in the church are facing?

More to Consider: Wiersbe writes, "If you and I refuse to obey God, either He can abandon us and get somebody else to do the job, and we will lose the reward and blessing, or He can discipline us until we surrender to His will." What is your reaction to this? Have you experienced or witnessed this? For biblical examples, read about Timothy, John Mark's replacement in the mission field (Acts 13:13; 15:36–41; 16:1–3), and about Jonah's discipline in the book of Jonah.

From the Commentary

From the human point of view, everything was against Esther and the success of her mission. The law was against her, because nobody was allowed to interrupt the king. The government was against her, for the decree said that she was to be slain. Her sex was against her, because the king's attitude toward women was worse than chauvinistic. The officers were against her, because they did only those things that ingratiated themselves with Haman. In one sense, even the fast could be against her; for going three days without food and drink would not necessarily improve her appearance or physical strength. But "if God be for us, who can be against us?" (Rom. 8:31 KJV).

The answer of faith is—"Nobody!"

—*Be Committed*, page 129

5. As you consider Esther's circumstances, why do you think she "stuck with the plan" even with everything against her? What are other examples

of this sort of persistence and trust (either from the Bible or your own experience)? What does this tell us about God's role in Esther's life (despite the absence of His mention in the book)?

From the History Books

There are plenty of stories about Christian servants who committed to a task that went against the current leadership and ended up as martyrs. These faithful followers were like Esther in their persistence of purpose, and in that everything was stacked against them. But unlike Esther, many of them were tortured and eventually killed for their boldness.

6. Why didn't Esther end up as a martyr? What is the difference between the stories of the martyrs and Esther's stand for her people? What implications does this disparity have for those who choose to stand up for their belief in Christ?

From the Commentary

> People may succeed for a time in covering up disgraceful
> activities, but eventually the truth surfaces, and everybody
> knows what's going on. And the culprit discovers that *the
> wrong we do to others, we do to ourselves.*
>
> The words of Psalm 7:14–16 make me think of Haman:
> "He who is pregnant with evil and conceives trouble gives
> birth to disillusionment. He who digs a hole and scoops it
> out falls into the pit he has made. The trouble he causes
> recoils on himself; his violence comes down on his own
> head" (NIV).
>
> —*Be Committed,* page 133

7. Wiersbe writes "eventually the truth surfaces." What is your reaction to
this? What are some examples of this? Was this "surfacing" a good thing or
a bad thing? What does this suggest about the importance of patience and
trust?

From the Commentary

> Let's note that Esther *prepared herself to meet the king.*
> (You'll recall that Ruth prepared herself to meet Boaz. See
> chap. 3.) If you knew you were going to meet the presi-
> dent of the United States at the White House, or royalty
> at Buckingham Palace, you would prepare for the meeting.
> Like Peter sinking into the sea, there are times when we
> have to rush into God's presence and cry out for help. But
> the power of those "emergency prayers" depends on our
> day-by-day fellowship with God, and that fellowship
> demands preparation. Preparing to pray is as important as
> the praying itself.
>
> —*Be Committed,* page 135

8. What does "preparing to pray" look like in Esther's story? How does
someone go about that today? Why is it so important?

From the Commentary

> Many theologians are of the conviction that pride is the
> very essence of sin. (Perhaps that's why pride is number
> one on God's "hate list." See Prov. 6:16–19.) It was pride
> that turned Lucifer into Satan: "I will be like the Most
> High" (Isa. 14:14 NKJV). Satan used pride to tempt Eve:
> "You will be like God" (Gen. 3:5 NIV). British Bible
> scholar William Barclay wrote, "Pride is the ground in
> which all the other sins grow, and the parent from which
> all the other sins come."
>
> —*Be Committed*, page 139

9. Circle some examples of Haman's pride in these chapters. What are other
examples of pride that led to a great fall? Do you agree that pride is the
essence of sin? Why or why not?

From the Commentary

> Malice is that deep-seated hatred that brings delight if our
> enemy suffers and pain if our enemy succeeds. Malice can

never forgive; it must always take revenge. Malice has a good memory for hurts and a bad memory for kindnesses. In 1 Corinthians 5:8, Paul compared malice to yeast, because, like yeast, malice begins very small but gradually grows and finally permeates the whole of life. Malice in the Christian's heart grieves the Holy Spirit and must be put out of our lives (Eph. 4:30–32; Col. 3:8).

The insidious thing about malice is that it has to act; eventually it must express itself. But when you shoot at your enemy, beware! For the ammunition usually ricochets off the target and comes back to wound the shooter! If a person wants to self-destruct, the fastest way to do it is to be like Haman and cultivate a malicious spirit.

—*Be Committed,* page 140

10. Think of examples of "malice" you've witnessed in your life (at work, at home, at school). In what ways did the person who had the malicious spirit get hit by the ricochet of his or her ammunition? Is this always the case? Why is malice so damaging for the person who holds it? What is a better response to have when you're angry about someone or something?

Looking Inward

Take a moment to reflect on all that you've explored thus far in this study of Esther 4—5. Review your notes and answers and think about how each of these things matters in your life today.

> *Tips for Small Groups: To get the most out of this section, form pairs or trios and have group members take turns answering these questions. Be honest and as open as you can in this discussion, but most of all, be encouraging and supportive of others. Be sensitive to those who are going through particularly difficult times and don't press for people to speak if they're uncomfortable doing so.*

11. Would you be confident enough in your faith to stand in "civil disobedience" if God asked you to? Why or why not? What are the greatest challenges you've faced where you've had to stand up for what you believe? What would it take to build confidence in your faith so you could stand up like Mordecai?

12. Look closely at the circumstances of your life—particularly those that have challenged your faith or upset you or confused you or even caused doubt. How might each of these be an example of God's providence at

work? Does knowing God is at work even in those circumstances give you comfort or does it unsettle you? Explain.

13. As you think about the things you've done that have hurt others, are there some that need to be "exposed"? Do you need to ask for forgiveness for wrongs done to others? If the truth always surfaces, what is the best way to deal with those secrets?

Going Forward

14. Think of one or two things that you have learned that you'd like to work on in the coming week. Remember that this is all about quality, not quantity. It's better to work on one specific area of life and do it well than to work on many and do so poorly (or to be so overwhelmed that you simply don't try).

Do you need to build your confidence in God so you can stand firmly when your faith is challenged? Do you need to develop patience so you can trust God is working things out for good? How will you do that? Perhaps you are feeling a specific prompting to live out some truth you've discovered in the Bible. Write these thoughts below. Be specific. Go back through Esther 4—5 and put a star next to the verse that is most encouraging to you. Consider memorizing this verse.

Real-Life Application Ideas: Read about the lives of Christian martyrs. What can you learn from these people of faith about the way God works in the lives of ordinary people? About God's timing? About the risks of standing firm in your faith?

Seeking Help

15. Write a prayer below (or simply pray one in silence), inviting God to work on your mind and heart in those areas you've previously noted. Be honest about your desires and fears.

Notes for Small Groups:

- *Look for ways to put into practice the things you wrote in the "Going Forward" section. Talk with other group members about your ideas and commit to being accountable to one another.*

- *During the coming week, ask the Holy Spirit to continue to reveal truth to you from what you've read and studied.*

- *Before you start the next lesson, read Esther 6—7. For more in-depth lesson preparation, read chapters 10 and 11, "Warning Signals" and "The Mask Comes Off," in* Be Committed.

The End of Haman's Rope
(ESTHER 6—7)

Before you begin …

- *Pray for the Holy Spirit to reveal truth and wisdom as you go through this lesson.*
- *Read Esther 6 —7. This lesson references chapters 10 and 11 in* Be Committed. *It will be helpful for you to have your Bible and a copy of the commentary available as you work through this lesson.*

Getting Started

From the Commentary

As much as we detest Haman and his foul deeds, we must keep in mind that God loves sinners and wants to save them. God is long-suffering and brings various influences to bear upon people's hearts as He seeks to turn them from their evil ways.

—*Be Committed,* page 146

1. What is your reaction to Wiersbe's statement? Is it easy for you to love someone like Haman? Why or why not? What were some of the influences God brought to bear on Haman's heart?

2. Choose one verse or phrase from Esther 6—7 that stands out to you. This could be something you're intrigued by, something that makes you uncomfortable, something that puzzles you, something that resonates with you, or just something you want to examine further. Write that here. What strikes you about this verse?

Going Deeper

From the Commentary

> While visiting the zoo, I became fascinated with the "noc-
> turnal exhibit." Here were animals that most of us never

see because they sleep in the daytime and do their active living at night. "While you are resting," said one of the posters, "Nature is busily at work helping to keep the balance of life stable." I thought to myself, *While I'm asleep, my heavenly Father is busily at work making sure the new day will be just what He wants it to be.* God's compassions never fail but are "new every morning" (Lam. 3:22–23) because God never sleeps and never stops working all things together for our good (Rom. 8:28).

— *Be Committed,* pages 146–47

3. How does it make you feel to know that "God never sleeps"? What are some examples of this in the book of Esther? In your own experiences at church, work, or home? How does this knowledge affect the way Christians ought to approach each day and each challenge?

From the Commentary

Can God direct us even in such minor matters as our recreations? He certainly can. When I was a young Christian, my attendance at a friend's birthday party turned out to be one of the most important events in my life. Because of that evening, I made a decision about my educational plans. That decision eventually led to my changing schools and meeting the girl who became my wife. Never underestimate the extraordinary things God can do through an ordinary event like a birthday party.

—*Be Committed,* page 147

4. Underline examples of God's direction in Esther's and Mordecai's stories. What are other examples of this you've witnessed or experienced? Is there a limit to how "small" God is willing to work in our lives? What's the difference between what Wiersbe describes in the excerpt and asking God to help you find a good parking spot at the mall, for example?

More to Consider: Wiersbe writes, "Is God in charge of schedules? He certainly is!" then lists examples of God's perfect timing. Read these yourself in Genesis 40:23—41:1 (the timing of Joseph as ruler) and Exodus 12:40–42 and Genesis 15:13–16 (the day the Jews left Egypt). What are other examples of God's timing?

From the Commentary

It has often been said that "God's delays are not God's denials." We sometimes get impatient and wonder why the wicked are prospering while the righteous are suffering, but God is never in a hurry. He is long-suffering toward the wicked because He wants them to repent, and He is patient with His people because He wants them to receive the right reward at the right time for the right purpose. If Mordecai was ever puzzled because the king promoted Haman but ignored him, he would soon find out that God had not made a mistake.

—*Be Committed*, pages 148–49

5. What are some examples of "God's delays" in Esther's story? What are some delays you or people you know are experiencing today? How might God be using these delays for His purposes?

From Today's World

Take a quick look at the most popular television series and movies that portray "good vs. evil." Popular media frequently portrays a hero as someone who arrives just in time to save the day. Good suspense is built on carefully crafted timing. If the hero arrives too soon, there's little excitement. But if he or she arrives too late, the bad guys win.

6. When you consider some of your favorite "hero saves the day" stories, what is it you like about these? How is the way popular media portrays heroes like or unlike the way the Bible portrays them? How is God's timing like or unlike the "just in time" approach of popular stories? What's unique about God's timing that doesn't fit the popular formula? How is Mordecai's story an example of this? Esther's? The Jewish people of their time?

From the Commentary

"Before destruction the heart of a man is haughty, and before honor is humility" (18:12 NKJV). The first half of that verse applies to Haman and the last half to Mordecai. What a difference a little comma makes! Proverbs 29:23 gives the same message: "A man's pride will bring him low, but the humble in spirit will retain honor" (NKJV). On which side of the comma do you live?

—*Be Committed,* page 150

7. Take a moment to review the characters of Haman and Mordecai. List their primary character traits. Now think about people you know who are on both sides of that "comma." What evidence of pride do you see in each of these people? What do you see as the cause of pride in those on the "Haman" side? The lack of pride for those on the "Mordecai" side?

From the Commentary

> Queen Esther bravely interceded for her people. How will the king respond? "Commit to the LORD whatever you do, and your plans will succeed. The LORD works out everything for his own ends—even the wicked for a day of disaster" (Prov. 16:3–4 NIV).
>
> —*Be Committed,* page 159

8. What gave Esther the confidence to intercede for her people? What does it mean to "commit to the LORD whatever you do"? How do you do that? What does it mean that "the LORD works out everything for his own ends"?

From the Commentary

> "Do not be deceived: God cannot be mocked," warned
> Paul. "A man reaps what he sows" (Gal. 6:7 NIV). Haman
> sowed anger against Mordecai, and he reaped anger from
> the king. Haman wanted to kill Mordecai and the Jews,
> and the king killed Haman. "Even as I have seen, they
> that plow iniquity, and sow wickedness, reap the same"
> (Job 4:8 KJV). "He who sows wickedness reaps trouble"
> (Prov. 22:8 NIV).
>
> —*Be Committed,* page 162

9. Describe some other examples (from Scripture and your own experience)
of the truth that you reap what you sow. What are some positive examples
of sowing and reaping? Some not-so-positive examples?

From the Commentary

> But let's keep in mind that this law of sowing and reap-
> ing also applies to doing what is good and right. If we
> sow to the flesh, we reap corruption, but if we sow to the
> Spirit, we reap life everlasting (Gal. 6:8). No good deed
> done for the glory of Jesus Christ will ever be forgotten

before God. No loving word spoken in Jesus' name will ever be wasted. If we don't see the harvest in this life, we'll see it when we stand before the Lord. Even a cup of cold water given in the name of Christ will have its just reward (Matt. 10:42; 25:31–46).

—*Be Committed*, page 163

10. Take a few moments to think of people who have sown good seeds but may not have seen the rewards on this side of heaven. What keeps someone pressing on toward the goal when rewards or even recognition are absent?

Looking Inward

Take a moment to reflect on all that you've explored thus far in this study of Esther 6—7. Review your notes and answers and think about how each of these things matters in your life today.

Tips for Small Groups: To get the most out of this section, form pairs or trios and have group members take turns answering these questions. Be honest and as open as you can in this discussion, but most of all, be encouraging and supportive of others. Be sensitive to those who are going through particularly difficult times and don't press for people to speak if they're uncomfortable doing so.

11. What are some of the challenges and trials you're facing today that you hope God is working on? How does the truth that "God never sleeps" help you as you consider these difficult times? What can you do to better handle your uncertainty with God's timing?

12. What is one time in your own life when God's delay caused you anxiety? When you saw the result (God's answer to your situation), how did that change your attitude? What are some practical lessons you can learn from previous stories of God's perfect timing?

13. What are some things you need to "commit to the Lord" and trust Him to work through? What are some things you can do to give God the "space to work" in those situations?

Going Forward

14. Think of one or two things that you have learned that you'd like to work on in the coming week. Remember that this is all about quality, not quantity. It's better to work on one specific area of life and do it well than to work on many and do so poorly (or to be so overwhelmed that you simply don't try).

Do you need to learn to trust God's timing? Do you need a greater confidence in God's care so you can stand tall when facing trials? Perhaps you are feeling a specific prompting to live out some truth you've discovered in the Bible. Write those thoughts below. Be specific. Go back through Esther 6—7 and put a star next to the verse that is most convicting to you. Consider memorizing this verse.

Real-Life Application Ideas: Speak with members of your church about the idea of God's timing. Interview them to learn how God has answered prayers according to His schedule and not theirs. You may also uncover some situations that are not yet "answered." Spend time with each person in prayer, asking for patience and trust that God's delay will not be God's denial.

Seeking Help

15. Write a prayer below (or simply pray one in silence), inviting God to work on your mind and heart in those areas you've previously noted. Be honest about your desires and fears.

Notes for Small Groups:
- *Look for ways to put into practice the things you wrote in the "Going Forward" section. Talk with other group members about your ideas and commit to being accountable to one another.*
- *During the coming week, ask the Holy Spirit to continue to reveal truth to you from what you've read and studied.*
- *Before you start the next lesson, read Esther 8—10. For more in-depth lesson preparation, read chapters 12 and 13, "From Victims to Victors" and "God Keeps His Promises," in* Be Committed.

Hope
(ESTHER 8—10)

Before you begin …
- *Pray for the Holy Spirit to reveal truth and wisdom as you go through this lesson.*
- *Read Esther 8—10. This lesson references chapters 12 and 13 in* Be Committed. *It will be helpful for you to have your Bible and a copy of the commentary available as you work through this lesson.*

Getting Started

From the Commentary

Haman was dead, but his murderous edict was still very much alive. Long after wicked people are gone, the consequences of their evil words and deeds live on. Even today, innocent people are suffering because of guilty people who lie in their graves.

—Be Committed, *page 167*

1. What is your immediate response to the king's inability to revoke the edict that doomed all Jews? What are other examples in history of the lingering consequences of an evil person's words or deeds?

2. Choose one verse or phrase from Esther 8—10 that stands out to you. This could be something you're intrigued by, something that makes you uncomfortable, something that puzzles you, something that resonates with you, or just something you want to examine further. Write that here. What strikes you about this verse?

Going Deeper

From the Commentary

> Everything that Haman had acquired from the king by his scheming, Mordecai received as gifts, because Mordecai

was a deserving man. At the beginning of this story, Esther and Mordecai were hardly exemplary in the way they practiced their religious faith, but now we get the impression that things have changed. Both of them have affirmed their Jewish nationality, and both were the means of calling all the Jews in the empire to prayer and fasting. In one sense, they spearheaded a Jewish "revival" and made being Jewish a more honorable thing in the empire.

God doesn't always give this kind of a "happy ending" to everybody's story. Today, not all faithful Christians are promoted and given special honors. Some of them get fired because of their stand for Christ! God hasn't promised that we'll be promoted and made rich, but He has assured us that He's in control of all circumstances and that He will write the last chapter of the story. If God doesn't promote us here on earth, He certainly will when we get to glory.

—*Be Committed*, pages 168–69

3. Take a close look at this "happy ending" to Esther and Mordecai's story. Was it free of strife? Why or why not? What sort of "fallout" was there in their story that wasn't all that "happy" after all? In what ways does the truth that God is in control help those who are suffering from consequences like these?

From the Commentary

> Esther's example encourages us to come to God's throne
> and intercede on behalf of others, especially the nations
> of the world where lost souls need to be delivered from
> death. *One concerned person devoted to prayer can make a
> great difference in this world, for prayer is the key that releases
> the power of God.* "Yet you do not have because you do not
> ask" (James 4:2 NKJV).
>
> —*Be Committed,* page 171

4. What sort of risk was Esther facing when she chose to stand up for her
nation? As you think about her story and the stories you see around you
today, what is your reaction to the claim that one person devoted to prayer
can make a great difference in this world? What does it mean to you that
"prayer is the key that releases the power of God"?

*More to Consider: According to Scripture, seventy-five thousand people
were slain by the Jews after the new edict was written allowing the Jews
to defend themselves. What is your immediate reaction to this? How is*

this like or unlike the way God protected the Jews from the Egyptian armies when Moses led them through the Red Sea?

From the Commentary

> We must pause and consider whether it was really ethical for Mordecai to give the Jews the authority to kill and loot. People who deny the divine inspiration of the Bible like to point to the various "massacres" in Scripture as evidence that the God of the Bible is "a bully." Imagine worshipping a god that commanded the slaughter of whole populations!
>
> —*Be Committed,* page 172

5. What are your reactions to Mordecai's decree? Do you believe it was God-inspired? Why or why not? Why didn't the king simply rescind the earlier edict? What does this story tell us about the cost of freedom?

From the History Books

If you study the genesis of the Crusades (1095–1291), you will find that the motivation for these Pope-sanctioned military operations was initially a desire to recapture Jerusalem and the "Holy Land" from Muslim rule. On the surface, this doesn't sound like a horrible goal, but over time, the targets of Christian zealots began to widen to include anyone considered a "heretic," and the methods for dealing with those who were not aligned with the church were anything but kind or humane.

6. What is the critical difference between the Crusades and the Jewish battles that killed seventy-five thousand supporters of Haman's original decree? Where was God during the Crusades? What does the comparison of these two events tell you about the importance of seeking God's will above all else? How might the Crusades have been affected had the church looked not to their own interests, but to God's desires for His people? Do you believe the church and those who promoted the Crusades believed God truly was leading them? What blinded them to the truth of God's will?

From the Commentary

The fear of God protects those who fear God and believe His promises. Because the Jews believed Mordecai's decree, they had new courage and were not afraid of the enemy, and their courage put fear into the hearts of the enemy. (See Phil. 1:28.) Before King Jehoshaphat went out to battle, God's message to him was: "Believe in the LORD your God, and you shall be established; believe His prophets, and you shall prosper" (2 Chron. 20:20 NKJV). That is still wise counsel.

—Be Committed, page 180

7. What does it mean to you to "believe in the LORD your God … [and] believe His prophets"? Does the second half of this apply today? Who are the prophets today we are to believe? If we do these things, we are told we'll prosper. What does that prosperity look like?

From the Commentary

The Jews in the other parts of the empire killed seventy-five thousand in one day, which shows how many people hated the Jews and wanted to destroy them. It averages out to about six hundred per province. Since the Jews were greatly outnumbered in the empire, their victory was certainly a tribute to their faith and courage.

—*Be Committed,* page 182

8. In what ways was the Jews' victory a tribute to their faith and courage? What would that faith and courage look like today? Where is it lived out? How?

From the Commentary

There's nothing wrong with *meaningful* tradition. The church is always one generation short of extinction, and if we don't pass on to our children and grandchildren what God has done for us and our fathers, the church will die of apathy and ignorance. "Come, my children, listen to me; I will teach you the fear of the LORD" (Ps. 34:11 NIV). It's when tradition gradually becomes *traditionalism* that we get into trouble.

—*Be Committed,* pages 183–84

9. What is the difference between "tradition" and "traditionalism"? Why is one a good thing and the other not? What is the "trouble" we get into when tradition becomes traditionalism? How do we avoid that trouble?

From the Commentary

> This brief chapter tells us that Mordecai, unlike his predecessor Haman, used his office to serve the king and help the Jews. Sometimes when people are elevated to high office, they forget their roots and ignore the needs of the common people. Mordecai wasn't that kind of man. Even though his political deeds are recorded in the official annals of the empire, what he did for his people has been recorded by the Lord and will be rewarded.
>
> —*Be Committed,* page 186

10. Can you think of examples from your own experience where someone was elevated to a high office and "forgot the little people," as it were? What causes people to lose sight of the needs of the common people? Why do so many campaign promises, for example, end up as nothing more than empty

wishes? How can we, as believers, stay focused on our roots in Christ when given positions of influence and power?

Looking Inward

Take a moment to reflect on all that you've explored thus far in this study of Esther 8—10. Review your notes and answers and think about how each of these things matters in your life today.

Tips for Small Groups: To get the most out of this section, form pairs or trios and have group members take turns answering these questions. Be honest and as open as you can in this discussion, but most of all, be encouraging and supportive of others. Be sensitive to those who are going through particularly difficult times and don't press for people to speak if they're uncomfortable doing so.

11. Think about the king's original edict and his inability to change that. Have you ever said something and then stuck by it even though it might have been wrong? What prompts this inflexibility? What impact would a true understanding of grace and mercy have on such rules?

12. What risks do you face as you live out your faith? Are you confident enough in your faith to stand up as Esther did, knowing full well your story might not have the same "happy ending"? Think about areas in your life where you are not particularly confident or strong—what can you do to build your faith there?

13. What are some examples of "prosperity" you have known because you believe in God and "His prophets"? What are the different kinds of prosperity followers receive? What is your response to the sort of prosperity God seems to be granting you (if any in this season)? Are you thankful? Disappointed? What does your answer to this question suggest about your relationship with God today?

Going Forward

14. Think of one or two things that you have learned that you'd like to work on in the coming week. Remember that this is all about quality, not quantity. It's better to work on one specific area of life and do it well than to work on many and do so poorly (or to be so overwhelmed that you simply don't try).

Do you need to develop a greater confidence in the way God is writing your story? Are there parts of the Esther story that you have difficulty with? What can you do to better understand this story and God's role in it? Perhaps you are feeling a specific prompting to live out some truth you've discovered in the Bible. Write these thoughts below. Be specific. Go back through Esther 8—10 and put a star next to the verse that is most convicting to you. Consider memorizing this verse.

Real-Life Application Ideas: It's often easy to dismiss difficult circumstances as nothing more than "the way it is." But what if God is intending to use those circumstances to grow your faith or perhaps even the faith of someone you know? Take a quick inventory of the challenges you're facing (especially those areas in life when your faith might be challenged by nonbelievers). Then talk with a friend about these circumstances and spend time in prayer asking God to reveal His purposes in them.

Seeking Help

15. Write a prayer below (or simply pray one in silence), inviting God to work on your mind and heart in those areas you've previously noted. Be honest about your desires and fears.

Notes for Small Groups:

- *Look for ways to put into practice the things you wrote in the "Going Forward" section. Talk with other group members about your ideas and commit to being accountable to one another.*
- *During the coming week, ask the Holy Spirit to continue to reveal truth to you from what you've read and studied.*

Summary and Review

Notes for Small Groups: This session is a summary and review of this book. Because of that, it is shorter than the previous lessons. If you are using this in a small-group setting, consider combining this lesson with a time of fellowship or a shared meal.

Before you begin ...
- *Pray for the Holy Spirit to reveal truth and wisdom as you go through this lesson.*
- *Briefly review the notes you made in the previous sessions. You will refer back to previous sections throughout this bonus lesson.*

Looking Back

1. Over the past eight lessons, you've examined two very different stories in the Bible that illustrate the creative ways God led women to make a difference in the world. What are the greatest biblical truths you've discovered in Ruth and Esther?

2. What is the most significant personal discovery you've made from this study?

3. What surprised you most about Ruth's story? Esther's story? What, if anything, troubled you? Spend some time in prayer about these things.

Progress Report

4. Take a few moments to review the "Going Forward" sections of the previous lessons. How would you rate your progress for each of the things you chose to work on? What adjustments, if any, do you need to make to continue on the path toward spiritual maturity?

5. In what ways have you grown closer to Christ during this study? Take a moment to celebrate those things. Then think of areas where you feel you still need to grow and note those here. Make plans to revisit this study in a few weeks to review your growing faith.

Things to Pray About

6. Ruth and Esther are packed with details that are specific to the culture of the time. But God is in these details just as He is in the overall message. Take a few minutes to pray that God would reveal to you just what He wants you to discover among all the facts and history offered in Ruth and Esther.

7. The messages in these two books focus primarily on trusting God and walking boldly in your faith. Take a few minutes to ask God to help you

trust Him more and become confident when faced with circumstances that might otherwise challenge your faith.

8. Whether you've been studying this in a small group or on your own, there are many other Christians working through the very same issues you discovered when exploring these books. Take time to pray for each of them, that God would reveal truth, that the Holy Spirit would guide you, and that each person might grow in spiritual maturity according to God's will.

A Blessing of Encouragement

Studying the Bible is one of the best ways to learn how to be more like Christ. Thanks for taking this step. In closing, let this blessing precede you and follow you into the next week while you continue to marinate in God's Word:

May God light your path to greater understanding as you review the truths found in the books of Ruth and Esther and consider how they can help you grow closer to Christ.

The "BE" series . . .

For years pastors and lay leaders have embraced Warren W. Wiersbe's very accessible commentary of the Bible through the individual "BE" series. Through the work of Cook International, the "BE" series is part of a library of books made available to indigenous Christian workers. These are men and women who are called by God to grow the kingdom through their work with the local church worldwide. Here are a few of their remarks as to how Dr. Wiersbe's writings have benefited their ministry.

"Most Christian books I see are priced too high for me . . .
I received a collection that included 12 Wiersbe
commentaries a few months ago and I have
read every one of them.
I use them for my personal devotions every day and they
are incredibly helpful for preparing sermons.
The contribution Cook International is making to the
church in India is amazing."

—Pastor E. M. Abraham, Hyderabad, India